The
Seven Rays

The Seven Rays

A Universal Guide to the Archangels

Samantha Stevens

INSOMNIAC PRESS

Copyright © 2003 by Samantha Stevens

All rights reserved. No part of this publication may be reproduced, stored in a retrieval system or transmitted, in any form or by any means, without the prior written permission of the publisher or, in case of photocopying or other reprographic copying, a license from Access Copyright, 1 Yonge Street, Suite 1900, Toronto, Ontario, Canada, M5E 1E5.

National Library of Canada Cataloguing in Publication Data

Stevens, Samantha, 1960-
    The Seven Rays: a universal guide to the Archangels / Samantha Stevens.

Includes bibliographical references.
ISBN 1-894663-49-7

1. Seven rays (Occultism). I. Title.

BF1442.S49S72 2003   133   C2003-904489-0

The publisher gratefully acknowledges the support of the Canada Council, the Ontario Arts Council and the Department of Canadian Heritage through the Book Publishing Industry Development Program. We acknowledge the support of the Government of Ontario through the Ontario Media Development Corporation's Ontario Book Initiative.

Printed and bound in Canada

Insomniac Press
192 Spadina Avenue, Suite 403
Toronto, Ontario, Canada, M5T 2C2
www.insomniacpress.com

This book is dedicated to the memory of Mary Westen... and to my Angels on Earth—Tom Smith, Nancy Upgren, Lydia Sirhawk, Antonio Gil, Deb Wheatley, Sybil Goldstein, Katherine Latanville, Ottilie Mason, Micheal Sabazeus, Caroline Benyes and Doc.

The author wishes to acknowledge a debt of gratitude and inspiration to the following truth seekers: Florence Scovell Shinn, Sanaya Roman, Elizabeth Clare Prophet and Osho.

Table of Contents

Chapter One
Why Talk to an Angel? — 9

Chapter Two
Making the Call — 37

Chapter Three
The Angels Within — 55

Chapter Four
The Angels Above — 65

Chapter Five
The Divine Rainbow — 85

Parting Thoughts — 93

Chapter One

Why Talk to an Angel?

Only fools rush in, where angels fear to tread... So why do so many of us insist on "going there"?

Earth is definitely a place that could be called a Fool's Paradise. Most of us are spiritual sociopaths who refuse to learn from our mistakes. The same bad things happen over and again to us, yet when pushed to account for our actions, we insist on blaming Fate. We are like a planet full of George Costanzas who can't understand why our actions almost always achieve the opposite of what we want in life.

We mistake the directives of our own egos for messages from God but ignore the big hints He gives us when we are following the wrong path. That is because we equate the surrender of ourselves to a Higher Power with defeat. We fear change, hate the word "no" and are addicted to the immediate gratification of our desires.

The worst of us treat the principles of spirituality like a chattel or a kind of debit point that we must use to expect a future reward. We throw a tantrum when we realize we will be earning our Air Miles in heaven. No wonder so many of us believe that "no good turn goes unpunished." "Turn the other cheek, get slapped twice!"

The world is filled with lonely, bitter people who carry the buds of cancer in their cells simply because they are unable to let go of resentments and grudges towards others. A law of the cosmos is that whatever is eating you will eventually consume you. We blame others for our mistakes and then weep and moan and rage when they don't like us for heaving guilt on them. Then we spend hours in psychiatrists' offices trying to rewrite the bad life script we wrote for ourselves in the first place (so it replays better in our heads) or try to obliterate accountability for our actions by loading up on self-negating antidepressants and prescription medications.

Most people do terrible things out of a fear of being unloved. Many channel their spiritual or physical energies into the destruction of those whom they feel unable to control—especially romantically. A common tendency is to refuse to respect the autonomy of others and refute their rights to make their own mistakes or choices in life. Sometimes we get angry at people because they won't let us treat them like porters who should be carrying our burdens for us. Your best course of action is to check your emotional baggage at the gates of Heaven in the first place.

Humans make this world a nice place to visit but a residential hell. We idealize and romanticize codependency and mistake negative attention-seeking for passionate love. We treat our soulmates and twin flames like slaves that were put here on Earth to take care of us, when really, that responsibility falls on the self. We mistake our own "desire to be desired" for true love, and rage when our own self-appreciation is not reflected back in our object of desire's eyes.

Some of us refuse to love at all. These individuals bank all of their sweetness, tenderness and kindness and selfishly save it all up for that one special person they might one day call a soulmate, while others around them starve for affection. I'm with Oprah on this one when she says, "Everybody is your soulmate." Even the guy at the corner store.

Most of us don't communicate with others. We merely communicate to people what we would like them to communicate back to us. We spend all day thinking, analyzing and sinking deeper and deeper into ourselves as others shrink and drift away in the same manner. We lose our spontaneity, ease and innocence as we are pulled deep into the muck of our unrequited desires. We become a repository of toxic psychic waste—unable to connect to others or to a higher wisdom.

It is time to realize that all is vain in love and war.

The problem is that we put all our faith and trust in humans that are as fallible as us, and then cry foul when they let us down. That is like putting your hand in the fire again and again and expecting not to get burned. The simple fact is humans make mistakes.

All of us are humans, all of us are fools and most of us need help.

That is why you want to make friends with an angel.

An angel is not human.

An angel always returns your call.

An angel can teach you to trust yourself.

An angel can help you "get out of self."

An angel can help you heal your injured instincts.

An angel can help you open your heart's center.

An angel can reconnect you with your Higher Self.

An angel will never lie to you.

Why waste your time getting bad advice from all these fools on Earth, when you can spend an evening socializing with a heavenly being?

An angel will always give you good advice.

However, an angel doesn't suffer fools gladly. That includes skeptics, those filled with spiritual pride, self-style martyrs, dangerous amateur shamans, budding witchlets and codependents looking for a supernatural parent. If you are reading this book because you think it will be your path to riches, control over others and total world domination, you and I are not on the same page.

This is a book about Soul Freedom.

Where do you see yourself living in the next year? In a Fool's Paradise, or in Heaven on Earth? An angel can help you look before you leap....

Everyone Is Psychic

One of the best lines I have ever heard about psychic integrity was in the movie *K-Pax*. A psychiatrist played by Jeff Bridges interviews a man who thinks he is alien, played by Kevin Spacey. The alien tells the psychiatrist that he comes from a planet where there are no laws. The psychiatrist then asks the alleged alien how people from his planet can tell the difference between right and wrong. The alien replies, "Don't be silly. Every creature is *born* knowing the difference between what is right and what is wrong."

It is this integral sense of knowing right and wrong coupled with the conviction that the universe is ultimately a benevolent place that is at the core of the development of intuitive abilities. You see this kind of wisdom reflected in the eyes and expressions of babies whose souls still express the innocence and purity of what Buddhists call the God-Head and others call the Divine Imagination. You could not imagine a baby intentionally hurting somebody. We are born with an innate sense of justice, fairness and respect for other living entities. We arrive here already knowing that everyone is connected to everyone else and that what hurts others also hurts the self.

You need to get back to the God-Head and rediscover your own sacred state of innocence.

It is the development of the ego and all of its desires and accompanying disappointments that eventually disconnects most of us from our innate psychic abilities. Some say the sixth sense disappears as the other five senses develop; others say that sixth sense is injured or damaged by abuse, neglect, frustration and rejection from others. Nobody on this earth escapes a crisis of faith, even if the crisis is as simple as that first lesson we all learn which is that "gravity sucks." It's an insult to the ego when the soother dropped on the floor refuses to magically fly back up and into our mouths again. It is the first time we think, "There is no God."

You don't need to be a professional psychic to connect to an angel, nor do you need to go to a channeller, medium, monk or a priest to connect to one. However, your ability to connect to the angels may depend to some extent on your ability to recoup that sense of the innocence of the Divine Imagination. You don't have to be a Zen master to do this. There are definitely some practical things you can do to enhance your psychic abilities:

- Meditate for ten minutes in the morning and ten minutes at night.
- Go for long walks in nature. Trees, rocks and water are particularly grounding and healing.
- Take baths in sea salt, to purify your aura and cleanse your energy centers.
- Practice creative visualization.
- Stop thinking or talking about yourself.
- Drop your grudges and resentments.
- Don't drink alcohol or do drugs.

That's it. It sounds easy, but most people stumble on that last one. Actually make that the last three! However, addiction is the number one symptom of injured instincts and the inability to connect to a Higher Power. Grudges and resentments also create huge astral blocks that can prevent you from accessing your Higher Self. Talking or thinking about yourself incessantly also functions as an astral block. You are like a radio that can only receive one station. You need to widen your broadband widths so you can receive additional channels.

The good news is that you don't have to be psychic at all to contact an angel. Angels don't judge people on how well they can meditate or how many drinks they have each day. They don't care if you have raped or murdered or lied or gossiped about the neighbor next door. The above seven suggestions however, might help you make that long distance call to the angels a clearer, more local connection.

Have you ever seen that bumper sticker "God Is My Psychic"? The principle is similar. Everyone is capable of making a direct connection with an angel. The Christian Buddhists call that psychic within the I Am That I Am. This concept has several sources, but it is what God called himself when Moses asked whose voice was emanating from the burning bush. The I Am That I Am is another name for the Divine Imagination, the God-Head, the Higher Power or Christ Consciousness. It symbolizes that pure innocence that allows you to connect your will to the will of the divine. It is the original angelic fire that inspires mankind to perform miracles on Earth.

Remember, you don't have to be psychic to contact an angel—they come to all who simply make the call with a humble heart.

Tales From the Psychic Line

Almost everyone has a story about sighting an angel, or being rescued at the last minute by "what must have been an angel." As a psychic who has read over fifteen thousand people in person, on the phone and in a popular chat room on the Internet, I have heard many stories about these mysterious, but helpful entities who seem to show up just in the nick of time to help or comfort those in trouble.

Many people initially experience the presence of an angel as some kind of light form. Some see the shadow of a human-shaped form that emanates light but is hollow in the center. A client and friend of mine, Mary, a channeller who was struggling with chemotherapy, often reported seeing this type just before her death from brain cancer. In her case, the human figure contained a flaming ruby-colored core and was surrounded by a pulsating gold and purple light. This sighting made us both sad, as we both knew that Uriel was the angel of letting go and that she was probably going to die. During that time she also saw a steely blue male form, with a pinpoint of bright white where his heart would theoretically be situated. Her description of this being, which arrived when she was in the most pain, fit the description of the Archangel Michael.

Others experience angels as a flood of light that fills the room with a definite omnipresence. Sometimes this light is like a flash, and other times it is more like the room has been shaded or brilliantly lit with a single tonal shade of color. One client mentioned this phenomenon while she was studying for a test. She had whipped herself up into a high state of anxiety about passing the examination when the room seemed to fill with a sunny light. The sudden arrival of this light, like the dawn of a new day, told me that she was being guided and protected by the Archangel Jophiel, the Angel of Illumination and Wisdom. She said that thanks to this light, she somehow found the focus and concentration to make it through the night.

Many people have also reported seeing sprays of light directed from a central spindle that spins upwards or downwards. Sometimes, these displays are what channellers call "just another light show" and sometimes they are messages from the beyond. I am not a grand authority on this subject but it is my belief this is some kind of healing vortex or energy download that is being sent from an angel to a suffering human being. Usually you can identify the angelic source responsible for the spiral by noting the color of the light. A white light signifies the guidance of Gabriel, the Angel of Guidance; yellow light indicates the arrival of Jophiel, the Angel of Illumination.

Another common report is the sighting of a ring or circle of light, hovering about six feet above a person that seems to consist of flaming flowers or a series of eyes. More often than not, people tell me they see this angel hovering above another person—usually a stranger. The sighting of this angel is so common that I have dubbed it the Angel of a Thousand Eyes. I am not so sure it is one angel, but maybe a legion of angels sent by the Archangel Jophiel, the Angel of Illumination. I believe it signifies that the person you are looking at has achieved some sort of enlightenment or is about to make a leap on the psychic path.

Sightings of wheels of light that appear to be flaming, rolling or spinning in the air are also common. This is similar to the "wheel within a wheel" that Ezekiel claimed he saw spinning through the air. The eyes or centers of the flowers often appear red in color and are surrounded by a honey-yellow glow. These sightings often occur in graveyards or near religious sites, and my assumption has been that these energy forms probably have something to do with the protective, loving energy of the Archangel Chamuel, the Angel of Love whose signature color is red.

Lightning bolts sighted around people or around oneself usually signify the presence of the Archangel Michael, the Angel of Protection. These zig-zag or triangular shapes are usually laser blue or white. One of my clients reported seeing these protective triangles around her children when they were riding their bikes in a silly way one day. Another reported seeing this around the office of her bank manager, who suddenly relented and gave her the loan that he originally denied her. One friend reported seeing this light around me after I returned from the hospital after being under general anesthesia. Being somewhat out of it, I am sure Michael sent some energy to protect me.

Quite a few people have commented on a flock of tadpole-shaped drops of light that appear to zip horizontally through the air in clusters. Once again, depending on the color, this wash of light probably indicates the movement of an Archangel in your presence or a flock of angels from a particular angel's legion.

Actual visual sightings of angels are less common than just the knowledge or sense that they are present.

Some people note a pleasant feeling accompanied by the sensation that they are being watched or that somebody is standing behind them. Many have claimed to feel an angel's hand on their forehead, stomach or heart. The hand is almost always described as cool to the touch. I have had this experience many times, particularly when I have had a fever. My first experience was when I was trapped in a fourth grade class that was boring me to tears. I prayed and prayed and prayed and one night, an ethereal blue-colored being seemed to float down from the stars outside my window, reach down, place its hand on my forehead and whisper "OK. Go to sleep." The next day my parents informed me that my teacher wanted me to skip a grade.

Others experience the angel as a disembodied voice that either shouts a command or whispers a suggestion into their ear. This is particularly common in the case of near car accidents, where a voice is heard to suddenly command "Turn left!" when a right turn would have led to certain death. The Archangel Michael is particularly responsive to the human voice. I have asked for his help and been assisted in all kinds of emergency situations. In one spectacular instance, I found myself shivering and unable to move or breathe as the result of an allergic reaction to an antibiotic. I called on the Archangel Michael for help and a friend appeared at the door and took me to the hospital. In another instance, I was cornered and pushed off my bike by a gang of adolescents who seemed intent on beating and robbing me. I called on the Archangel Michael for help, imagining myself surrounded by his steely blue white light, and the leader of the gang ordered his cohorts to leave me alone.

Some angels make their presence known by an odor; many announce themselves by filling the room with the scent of roses, lilies, cedar, sandalwood or freshly cut grass. If you are smelling roses and seeing rainbows at the same time, it is a sure sign that something great is about to happen. Roses often signify the presence of Archangel Chamuel and his angels of love.

Angels also make their presence known through the phenomenon of coincidence; when the same message or image appears to be reflected again in diverse media. For example, the phrase "Stop thinking about tomorrow" is constantly conveyed to you in a two or three day span in music lyrics, images on television, as a newspaper headline or on billboards. You may hear this message from out of the mouths of babes, madmen, people begging for quarters on the street and as part of conversation with friends and family alike. Coincidences or synchronicity like this are often what drive an individual to contact a psychic to determine whether or not these messages are from a divine place, a psychic vampire or simply the product of indigestion.

There is a fine line between obsession and receiving divine messages from an angel. Those with injured instincts, like women who are addicted to abusive relationships or who are in codependent relationships, often see their oppressor as the "angel" in their lives who is giving them the messages. Although it is true that some people do act as vessels or conductors for the actions of angels, an abuser is rarely their conduit of choice. The woman who thinks she is receiving divine messages from her ex often thinks that because she has confused romantic love with

Divine love. The reason she is so desperate to get the bad guy back is because the romance represents her connection with God. We are taught to see The Other, The Lover, as the divine messenger—an angel—sent to us from God. Codependents often dehumanize their lovers by placing these angelic expectations on them. It is crucial to realize that you don't need a lover, a priest or medium to connect with the higher realms. You can do it yourself.

However, there are definitely instances where a complete stranger seems to appear out of nowhere and help you when you are in trouble. One client of mine was completely broke as a result of being stiffed on child support and could not feed her children. She was walking along the street, praying fervently in her heart for God to help her, when a stragglylooking man with a long white beard began to follow her. At first she tried to avoid him, because she thought he was a street person about to ask her for money. She was shocked when he pressed a roll of twenties in her hand. When she looked up to thank him, he was gone.

Angels also make their presence known through a phenomenon known as *spontaneous manifestation*. When you need something that you have been wishing for and then it miraculously appears, that is usually the work of an angel. I have had this personally happen many times with money. I have often called to the Archangel Raphael (who is the angel responsible for keeping food on the table), and the next day have had an editor call and assign me a story with an advance for exactly the amount of money I need, or opened my mailbox to find a check for an unexpected royalty or refund.

Another client of mine, who is a recovering heroin addict, described how she was broke and had lost everything as a result of her actions. She was truly remorseful and prayed to the angels for help. She knew she had twenty dollars in her bank and when she went to the ATM to draw it out, the machine mysteriously spit out more than the needed amount.

It seems that the angels believe that love is an action. Sightings of angels and physical contact are much rarer than seeing the results of your prayer manifest in real life.

The Divine Rainbow

There are thousands of angels, named by thousands of religions in the angelic pantheon. The angels described in this book are based on Buddhist and Christian theories about the Seven Rays and how these energies correspond to the physical body, the auric body and the archangels. I have chosen the Seven Rays as a model to introduce you to the seven most universal angelic entities. The Rays or Divine Flames (as they are sometimes called) represent elements in the perfectly integrated human being—one whose heart is aligned with their will and inspired by the Divine Imagination.

These are the Seven Rays, or the Angels Within:
• The First Ray represents Divine Will and survival, and is associated with the colors red and blue.
• The Second Ray represents Inner Wisdom and sexuality, and is associated with the colors gold and orange.
• The Third Ray represents Unconditional Love and communication, and is associated with the colors gold, yellow and pink.

- The Fourth Ray represents Harmony and the ability to give and receive Love. It is represented by the colors pink, red and green.
- The Fifth Ray represents Knowledge and self-expression, and is represented by the colors blue and white.
- The Sixth Ray represents Peace and the sixth sense, and is represented by the colors magenta and violet.
- The Seventh Ray represents Soul Freedom and the ability to receive divine guidance from the Higher Self. It is represented by the color violet.

These rays, in turn, also correspond to energy centers in our body, known as *chakras*. The chakras are different colored energy centers that originate from seven different points in our body. Chakra is a Sanskrit (East Indian) word that means "wheel." In essence, chakras are wheels of light. For millennia, the chakras have been imagined as round balls, blossoms or spheres of light that can open, close, darken, brighten and spin. The location of each of the seven chakras represents a different aspect of human experience. Emotions, ability to connect with others and physical health are thought to be reflected in the condition of each chakra.

Seeing your own chakras requires mental focus and powers of meditation. Remember these are imaginary entities that were invented by great mystics millions of years before medical technology. The manipulation of these spheres or wheels of light, particularly the brightening and opening of them, was thought to relieve a variety of ailments.

There are seven main chakra centers in the human body which correspond with the seven colors of the rainbow or light spectrum. I have also named the primary corresponding Archangel.

The Red Chakra, also often referred to as the root, first or base chakra is at the base of the trunk of the body. It is also believed to rule our primal drives—the desire to procreate, survive and destroy. This is the chakra to work on if you are having troubles with your health. It is connected to the First Ray and the Archangel Chamuel, the Angel of Joy.

The Orange Chakra, sometimes called the second, sexual or spleen chakra is in the abdomen and relates to the lower digestive organs. It corresponds to our ability to physically digest and eliminate food, and emotionally digest events and process them in a healthy way. It further relates to emotions such as joy or affection. This is the chakra to work on if you are having trouble letting go or suffering from post-traumatic stress disorder. It is connected to the Second Ray and the Archangel Jophiel, the Angel of Illumination.

The Yellow Chakra, sometimes called the third, stomach or solar plexus chakra, is located in the upper stomach area just below the rib cage. It is the center where we connect to others on an astral level, and it relates to our ability to transform or manifest events. It connects to the Third Ray and the Archangel Gabriel, the Angel of Guidance.

The Green Chakra is located in the chest and is related to the lungs and heart. It is sometimes called the fourth or heart chakra, and represents the flow of energy, love and communication in our lives. This is the Fourth Ray. The Green Chakra is also related to the Archangel Raphael, the Angel of Healing.

The Blue Chakra, sometimes called the fifth, thyroid or throat chakra relates to the immune system, and the regulation of hormones. It represents our ability to communicate effectively with others, and denotes creative and personal expression. This is the Fifth Ray. It is related to the Archangel Michael, the Angel of Truth and Protection.

The Indigo Chakra, sometimes known as the sixth chakra or the Third Eye, is located just slightly above and between the eyebrows on the forehead, and connects to the pituitary gland. This chakra guides mental and spiritual processes, and helps develop intuition and second sight. This is the Sixth Ray. It is related to the Archangel Uriel, the Angel of Peace.

The Seventh Chakra, also sometimes known as the crown, violet, white or lotus chakra, is located at the top of the head. It is thought to be the gateway or connection to the spirit world and the Higher Self. It is the receptor of divine wisdom and inspiration. This is the Seventh Ray, also known as the Violet Flame or Violet Ray. It is related to the Archangel Zadkiel, the Angel of Joy.

When functioning well, the chakras are thought to be a conduit for the constant flow of energy throughout our bodies. If these chakras are blocked, stilled, darkened or not working, then you can imagine them being cleared from negative energies such as resentment, fear or trauma. Tuning up your chakras can make an enormous difference to your sense of well-being. Chakras that are blocked are thought to cause physical disease and emotional and spiritual dis-ease. Common blockages that originate from negative emotions are the desire to hurt, being emotionally hurt, the holding on to of fears and resentment and sometimes past life issues. The chakras interact with each other in a perpetual dance of the spheres that extends outside our bodies. They exist in a constant state of renewal that can be enhanced by meditation, creative visualization, light working and breath work.

When under astral attack, these chakras can be "hooked" into or captured by another's invasive energy. Usually this energy is a living person, who for some reason has a damaged aura. Primary damage to the aura is caused by something physical—drug addiction, brain damage, trauma or a chemical brain imbalance. The mentally ill or drug addicted can be powerful, natural channellers. Many of them have subconsciously developed superior sixth senses as a compensating or predatory mechanism that makes up for the damage done to their minds and souls. They depend on the energies of others for survival. As they are unable to subsist on their own energies, they become expert astral attackers that attach and hook onto others. The most popular sites of attack are the solar plexus, heart, throat and crown chakras. A psychic will tell you that these invasions often look like a thread or cord with a hook on the end. Some attackers, especially Buddhists gone wrong, picture an astral shard or hologram of themselves and astrally plant it in the appropriate chakra. In the post-*Celestine Prophecy* age, this is what I define as pure evil.

An attack on the solar plexus center can prevent you from connecting to anyone but the attacker. An invaded heart chakra can make it difficult for you to free yourself so you can love others. People who have trouble expressing themselves often have a hook in their throat chakra—their voice feels strangled in their throat. Individuals who believe that an obvious oppressor is their soulmate are being attacked in their crown center. When you feel that someone has you by the short and curlies they are most likely attacking you in your sexual base and second chakra centers.

The chakras are also instruments that you can use to call or connect to the various angels. They are like tuning forks that cause another energy to vibrate in resonance with your own energy. The idea is to keep them healthy, brilliant and clear so that they will resonate with a higher frequency.

You wouldn't ask a plumber to fix your computer, so it is important to know which archangel is best at fixing which kind of problem. Each angel has a job, and exists on an astral plane that corresponds to one of the seven rays in the divine rainbow. In turn, these rays or flames correspond to a different energy center in our body.

Here is a concise list of the Seven Archangels, their functions and corresponding places in the Divine Rainbow:

The ARCHANGEL MICHAEL is the ANGEL OF PROTECTION. His main color is blue. You can connect to him through the base, solar plexus, throat and crown chakras. Michael takes care of issues related to the First, Third, Fifth and Seventh rays. Practically, you can ask him and his legions of light for protection from any kind of physical or spiritual danger. This includes accidents and attacks of all kinds including traffic accidents, stalkers, robbers, as well as spiritual threats such as astral attack, witchcraft and the evil eye. Spiritually, he can help restore your faith in God and free you from fear and self-doubt. He also protects soldiers and the leaders of government.

The ARCHANGEL CHAMUEL is the ANGEL OF LOVE and corresponds to the color pink. You can connect to him through the base, second, solar plexus and heart chakras. Chamuel takes care of issues related to the First, Second, Third and Fourth rays. This is the angel of compassion, mercy, forgiveness and understanding. This angel helps you repair damaged relationships and make new friends. Pray to this angel if you need to find a lost object, have money problems or need to find a new job. Chamuel's pink ray can also help dissolve feelings of self-condemnation, guilt and low self-esteem.

The ARCHANGEL RAPHAEL is the ANGEL OF HEALING and corresponds to the color green. He rules the base, heart and throat chakras and relates to the First, Fourth and Fifth rays. Raphael is responsible for the healing of body, mind, soul and spirit and can help when you are in need of clothing, food or shelter. Raphael can also help doctors make the right decisions and aspiring musicians make beautiful music. Spiritually, this angel repairs broken bodies and spirits, and helps you accept the truth.

The ARCHANGEL GABRIEL is the ANGEL OF GUIDANCE . His color is white. You connect to him through the base, second, solar plexus and crown chakras. He corresponds to the First, Second, Third, Fifth and Seventh rays. This angel can help you organize and streamline your life, as well as provide you with advice on your education and career. This is also the angel you pray to if you need an item for your home, such as a stove or a fridge. Spiritually, Gabriel helps you find your life purpose and replaces feelings of discouragement with joy and fulfillment.

The ARCHANGEL JOPHIEL is the ANGEL OF ILLUMINATION and corresponds to the color yellow. You connect to him through the second, solar plexus, heart, Third Eye and crown chakras and the Second, Third, Fourth, Fifth, Sixth and Seventh rays. This angel can help free you and loved ones from addictions, improve memory, help you pass tests and retain information and knowledge. Spiritually, he can help you connect with your Higher Self and show you the way when it comes to making difficult decisions. This is the angel who exposes secrets and lies, and helps fight pollution on the planet.

The ARCHANGEL URIEL is the ANGEL OF PEACE and corresponds to the colors purple and gold. He rules the second, solar plexus, heart, throat, Third Eye and crown chakras. Uriel relates to the Second, Third, Fourth, Fifth, Sixth and Seventh rays. He resolves all problems in personal, social and professional relationships, and helps to create harmony in your life. He is the angel of nurses, doctors, counsellors and teachers. He can help you to let go of bitterness and resentment. He renews hope in hearts that have lost faith. He is also the angel who manifests divine justice in courtrooms.

The ARCHANGEL ZADKIEL is the ANGEL OF JOY and corresponds to the color violet. He corresponds to the second, heart, throat, Third Eye and crown chakras; the Fourth, Fifth and Seventh rays. This is the angel to pray to if you need work as an actor, writer or performer. He is also the angel of architects and engineers. Zadkiel is the angel you pray to if the kids are fighting or if your computer won't reboot. Zadkiel stands for freedom, happiness, justice, mercy and freedom of the soul.

The Structure of the Etheric Body—The Fountain of Light

Every human being is thought to be surrounded by an etheric body, also known as the *aura*. This energy field is thought to be made up of the emanations of your life force—what the Middle Eastern religions call *prana*, the Chinese call *chi* and the Western religions call the *soul*. An entire New Age cottage industry has sprung up around the idea of taking electromagnetic pictures of these phenomena using Kirlian or electromagnetic photography. Psychics and channellers take cues from the colors revealed in these photographs to diagnose and interpret physical, spiritual and emotional conditions.

The most prominent element of the etheric body, or *soul-structure* as it is also known, is said to consist of the aura itself. Typically, the aura extends about three feet around the physical body in all directions. It often resembles a bubble of light that is sealed by a slightly thicker membrane that preserves the autonomy of the entity. Imagine a soap bubble filled with light and you get the idea. Some people have larger, more expansive auras, and often you can recognize these people by the way they seem to mysteriously fill a room with their presence. Others have auras that seem to extend as far as six feet above their head. This elongation of the aura, towards the skies and the realms of the ascended masters, saints and angels, is a goal of many devoted Buddhists, Christians and spiritual seekers.

All the chakras play important roles in maintaining the health of the aura, but the one directly involved in communication with angels is the crown chakra. Above the crown chakra is the source of what is usually called the Higher Self, Divine Imagination or the center of Christ Consciousness, typically seen as a small sun or ball of shining light that emanates rays downward. In order for this light to emanate, the crown chakra has to be open to receive what the Buddhists call enlightenment.

One way to understand the chakra system is to imagine that there is a string of multicolored Christmas lights connected from your base chakra up through your body to the crown of your head. Connected to that is an extension cord that further plugs into this power source six feet above you. The idea is to send light up those bulbs by plugging into your energy source. That ball of light above your head is what talks to other souls and angels on your behalf. It sends messages to your chakras that in turn deal with issues of survival, sexuality, communication, your ability to give or receive love, self-expression, second sight and the ability to receive divine guidance. If you manage to plug into this higher source and light up all your chakras, you are said to have awakened your *kundalini* (the Buddhist name for an upward spiral of energy).

The ball of light known as the Higher Self, the Divine Imagination or the center of Christ Consciousness relates strongly to the heart chakra, which is seen as a pinpoint of light. The third chakra, at your diaphragm, is used to energize the heart chakra each time you take a breath inside your body. Energizing the third and fourth chakras by controlling the breath is thought to open the crown chakra so that it can receive the light and wisdom of the messages sent from the Higher Self to the physical body. This pathway forms a kind of circuitry that energizes and strengthens your connection to your Higher Self and the angels.

To open your crown chakra, try the following simple basic exercise:

Breathe in, and as you do, imagine the white sunny ball of fierce bright light, the Higher Self Sun, hovering six feet about your head.

Now imagine that there is another sunny ball of yellow light glowing in your upper tummy (your solar plexus).

As you breathe out imagine the Higher Self Sun shooting a saber-like beam of light, straight down through the crown to energize this ball of light in your solar plexus.

For the next ten breaths, imagine energy shooting up from your solar plexus area to the sun above your head as you inhale, and the energy shooting back down with each exhale. Imagine your entire stomach area filled with a brilliant, honey-colored, warm light.

Now imagine your heart's center as a small, pink pinpoint of light.

Each time you breathe in, your solar plexus reaches for that energy from the Higher Self Sun in the sky. Now when you breathe out, the super-charged solar plexus chakra sends energy back towards your heart center. The pinpoint of light in your heart is like a small shining star that gets brighter and larger with each breath. You are feeding the heart's center, using the solar plexus chakra as a conduit for the energy from the Higher Self.

With each breath out, this pinpoint of light in your heart chakra grows brighter and brighter and larger and larger... until it starts to resemble a little fountain.

This fountain shoots white light upwards, higher and higher, releasing a spray of light that falls from your crown to your feet. Every time you breathe out, your body is showered in a spray of rainbow-colored lights. Imagining a fountain of diamonds is always good.

Now, each time you breathe, the following sequence should be taking place: you inhale and send solar plexus energy up through the crown of your head to the Higher Self Sun six feet above your head. You exhale and the Higher Self sends energy down to the solar plexus which, in turn, sends energy to the heart's center. This energy explodes in a fountain of light that circulates to the top of your head, showers to your feet then rises again.

With each breath, you are now rinsing yourself with holy light from the Higher Self.

This is an efficient way of opening your chakras and increasing your receptivity to messages from the angels.

You Are the Divine Vessel

There are many clichés available to describe the concept of the Divine Vessel. Perhaps the oldest is "the body is the temple of soul." Look inside your temple. Who lives there? How many unwanted tenants do you have in there? Is it a residential hell filled with the astral imprints, toxic parents, moneylenders, warmongerers, addicts, martyrs and other fools on Earth? Time for an eviction.

Who built your temple? Did you build it yourself or have others build it for you from the debris left over from a devastating experience? Think back. When you think of your life over the past ten, thirty or sixty years, what would you name as your most life-defining moments? The worst experiences in your life, or the best? Most of us have temples shaped by the wind's negative forces—our own and others.

This is important because ultimately, we are constructed in the image of our Higher Self. Recall the concept of I Am That I Am. The answers you are looking for are ultimately within. Angels are merely messengers. Being humans, we like to kill the messenger. You are the main inhabitant of your temple and your job is to make it a nice place for the angels to visit.

Another way to describe this divine vessel is as a cup. The cup is made up of your personality. Personality embraces the ego. The idea is to empty this cup of ego and fill it with the divine light from the Higher Self. This is done by a process that can only be described as an astral evaporation known as "surrendering up." You ask your Higher Power to take all the gunk in the cup and send it up to be transformed into positive energy. This is called *transmutation*—the transformation of negative energy into positive energy.

Another way of picturing the Divine Vessel is as a computer. Your crown chakra is the download manager. When you contact the angels you are asking for wisdom to be downloaded from your Higher Self into the appropriate chakra, or file.

Some channellers, psychics, healers, priests and mediums eventually develop the ability to open your crown chakra, contact your Higher Self and spiritually download this information for you. However, I strongly recommend you do this for yourself. In fact, I would stay away from anybody who offers to open your crown chakra or who you suspect may be trying to do you such a favor. You are a natural entity capable of receiving your own information in the right doses at the right time. Sudden accelerations on the spiritual path are dangerous. The reason so many channellers, mediums and psychics seem like such complete crackpots is because they are. They have literally cracked their personality container by filling it with more light than it can hold, and as a result, have developed all kinds of disorders.

Like every other part of your life, only you are responsible and accountable for the integrity and health of your inner spiritual landscape.

Picture a cup. What does it look like? Is it a cracked earthenware vessel or does it look like the Holy Grail? Picture it being emptied of stagnant tears, poisoned emotions and the dregs of past disappointments. Revisualize it as a shining, golden goblet, that is open and willing to receive...

Chapter Two

Making the Call

How to Pray

An angel can be your best friend. These cosmic beings, especially Michael, have been known to respond to urgent requests for help from those who are in immediate danger or great pain. A verbal request such as "Somebody up there please help me!" is called a *fiat*. However, the angels seem to respond the fastest when they are addressed politely by their Christian names.

An angel is to be treated like a friend or an equal, as opposed to a servant or slave to your desires. Angels don't like to be bossed around. They tend to steer away from those who are drunk with arrogance or spiritual pride and flock to those who are humble or genuinely in a state of true surrender. They also respond immediately to tears, as it is said "tears are prayers without words."

Angels are to be treated like guests who are invited into your heart. Like most guests, they tend to leave or ignore environments that are filled with aggression, anxiety, anger and hostility. So before you call on an angel, it is important to meditate, and picture your heart or fourth chakra as a tender, peaceful and welcoming place… the kind of place you'd want to stay for a while if you were an astral being. Before you call on an angel to do you a favor, it is important to imagine your heart as a temple that honors these benevolent beings.

The first thing you must do when you call upon an angel is prepare your heart to receive its presence. Lighting a candle that corresponds to the Angel's color can help you connect to that particular angel's ray, but it is not necessary. Speak the angel's name out loud. Talk to the angel like you would a treasured confidante. Please don't treat an angel like an authoritarian. An angel is not to be mistaken for a cruel parent or an evil fairy that might not grant your wish. Don't demand immediate gratification and don't be so rude as to interrupt if you start to hear a message that doesn't fit with your ego or lust-based desires.

It is also important not to attach a sense of panic or anxiety to your prayers or requests. The fact that you feel this way represents a lack of faith in the universe and can often create the opposite effect. For instance, if you phrase a prayer like this: "I need more money," you might just create a number of situations where you need more money. Prayers are like affirmations. Keep your language in the present tense and use a phrasing that is a statement that your wish has already been granted.

Also, be careful what you pray for, especially when you pray for others. Pray for their highest good, as opposed to what you think is best for them. In this instance, ignorance truly is bliss.

It is also important to end each prayer with the request that all of those on the planet with the same need as you be granted their requests.

End the prayer with an expression of gratitude, for all the things you already have and for the blessings you are about to receive in the future.

If you are silent, respectful, fervent and loving, an angel will always give you the answer you need to solve your problem.

Make your request specific, and visualize what you would like if you can, but don't be attached to the outcome. Angels are agents of the Higher Power and like God, they work in mysterious ways.

Mental Hygiene—You Can't Cure Mind with Mind

When confronted with a problem, most of us try to analyze, strategize or think our way out of the situation. The more we obsess about finding a solution, the more we create additional anxiety. In astral terms, anxiety has a low, base vibration, which only intensifies itself. Vibrations tend to cluster together like a forest of tuning forks. Before you know it, you have created more anxious situations and more people in your life who express a similar anxious desperation. The buildup of this anxiety can act as a block to accessing your Higher Power. This is what is called "getting in your own way."

Believe it or not, you are in control of your own mind. You can choose your thoughts, feelings and reactions, and train your imagination. Many people insist this is not possible. Many find it an incredible concept—almost an imposition. It is OK to tell your mind to shut off. Enough is enough. Unfortunately, "the mind run riot" can be defined as a form of insanity. If you are not master of that domain called your brain, who is?

The best way to clear the mind of this bad habit is to rid it of all thoughts. This is best done through the process of meditation.

Here is a simple meditation based on a Tibetan mind-clearing ritual:

Lie down on your bed and focus on a spot on the wall. Stare at the spot and breathe deeply, making sure the inhalations and exhalations are coming from your stomach area. Don't take shallow breaths. One way to tell is to notice whether or not your stomach is moving up and down or if your chest is moving up and down. If your chest is moving, you are not breathing correctly in order to meditate. Breathe from your belly.

Now, relax all of your muscles from head to toe. One way to do this is to clench all of your muscles for a few seconds and then let go. Start with clenching your toes and then let go. Move on to your calves. Clench your calves and then let go. Work your way up your body doing this with each muscle group until you feel completely relaxed.

Now pretend you are dead. Feel yourself getting so heavy that you couldn't move a muscle, even if you tried. Feel yourself getting cold. Don't move a muscle, not even your eyes. If you try to move a muscle, you can't. It is as if you are paralyzed. Continue to stare at the spot on the wall.

As you do this, you may notice a few thoughts floating up before your mind's eye. Just note them, by saying to yourself, "That's a thought," and then dismiss it. As each thought arises, greet it and dismiss it: "Goodbye thought! You are just a thing! Form without content."

After a while, you will begin to notice that you are having no thoughts at all. Continue staring at the wall as long as you can, without effort or strain and lying as still as you can. You will soon find yourself in a state that is conducive to true meditation. Your mind will become blank and your breathing deep and slow. Do nothing.

Congratulations. You have emptied your Divine Vessel. You are now ready to fill your loving cup with light from the angels. This is a good time to pray and ask for what you want.

Emotional Hygiene—The Angels Won't Enter a Messy Temple

Believe it or not, you are also in control of your emotions. You can choose your reactions to events in the past, present or future. Many people find this an outrageous concept as they see themselves as being at the mercy of other people. Others don't really have the power to make us happy and sad. Yet most of us give all our power to the same sorry, fallible people that live in the Fool's Paradise described in Chapter One.

Many people make the mistake of believing that their feelings are reflections of reality. If you think this, then that is unfortunately another instance of insanity. Reality seen through the filter of your feelings is like looking into a fun-house mirror—what is reflected back is warped with resentment or bloated with fear.

You have to look into the darkest chambers of your heart and ask yourself who is living there. To whom have you given the power to make you happy or sad? Who have you been resenting for years? Who do you fear? Present these tenants with an eviction notice. Take your power back. Decide that you are proactive, not reactive. Reactive people are terminal victims and martyrs.

One way to do this on a daily basis is to practice the credo of "change the thought, change the feeling." Feeling sad about that time your boyfriend lit your hair on fire? Change the thought and your feeling will change. Thoughts from our mind are like little keys that open doors to rooms filled with the remnants of the past. Practice a little Feng Shui on your heart. Clear the clutter. Rearrange the furniture. Picture your feelings as bouquets of flowers. Replace dying bouquets of flowers with new ones. Make your Divine Vessel a nice place for the angels to visit.

Another one of my favorite, yet cryptic clichés is the phrase "It's not about you." This forces you to take the perspective that you can't take everything that happens to you personally, because ultimately what other people do is not about you. It is about them. You are about you. You are not about what some person did to you last year or twenty years ago. You are about what you do to yourself. And right now you are going to invite the angels into your heart. You are going to walk and talk with them and ask for divine guidance about how to deal with these fools on Earth.

Prayers or wishes that are attached to extreme emotions tend to achieve the opposite effect, although some would argue that great displays of grief or even self-abuse while praying guarantees greater results. The Cosmos in general does not appear to smile on drama queens. Beseeching, wailing, throwing tantrums and making demands does not seem to convince the angels of anything except the fact that you seem resistant to suggestion. You are so convinced, that you cannot be convinced of anything else. If it smacks of effort, it is not going to work. You might, however, get a job acting in a soap opera.

It is the simplest of requests that work best. Don't agonize, don't justify and don't explain while you pray. If you attach anxiety to the prayer, the opposite will manifest. If it helps, pretend that you have the innocence of a small child, who is making her first wish upon a star. That is the kind of purity of intention that is required in a conversation with an angel.

What to Say When You Pray

I am a big believer in the strength of a personal prayer. However, I have created a guide below for those of you who prefer to follow a structured format. This Universal Prayer to the Angels can be used to address any of the seven archangels. It is based loosely on Elizabeth Clare Prophet's prayer structure, which I have found to be extremely effective.

It is OK to follow the structure below and write your prayer down and read it. It is also good to read your prayer out loud if you choose to use this more formal method.

First, clear your mind. Try to be as relaxed as possible.

Light a candle that is appropriate. Though optional, you can find more about using candles as a prayer aid in the next chapter.

First you call all the angels…

"In the name of ____" (insert one of the following—the one that feels best to you:) **The God or Goddess That Is Within Me, The Divine Imagination, My Higher Power, The Great Being of Light or The I Am That I Am.**

"I call to all the seven archangels and their legions of light. I ask that all Seven Rays bless me with their divine guidance."

Then you call the specific angel. For the purposes of this exercise we are going to use the Archangel Michael.

"I call on the Archangel Michael and his legions of light. I ask for their protection."

Then you make general requests that address the overall nature of the issues that replace all negatives with positive:

"I ask the angels for protection against losing my car and my job. I ask the angels to be free of anxiety and filled with emotional security. I ask that they replace my lack of confidence with the ability to stand up for myself. I ask that all doubts about the future be replaced with faith so that no matter what happens, all will be well."

At this point in the prayer you may also visualize the chakra that is associated with the angel. Michael is related to the fourth chakra of self-expression so you may want to visualize your heart center glowing a brilliant blue. If this is too much for you to handle at first, just concentrate on getting the words right.

Then you make a specific request and describe specific situations that you would like fixed. For example: "I ask the angels to please resolve my problem at work and protect me from job loss. I ask the angels to please help me find the money to fix the brakes on my car so I don't have an accident."

Then explain to the angels why *you* think the fulfillment of your request would be good for all. Example: "I ask that this be done because it would be bad news for everyone if I lost my job right now. I ask that my brakes be fixed as I can't get to work without the car and I need to go to work!"

Then you ask for more general qualities associated with the angel. Name anything that comes to mind that is associated with this angel and things *will* come to mind. Wish for improvements in the entire world.

Example for Michael: "I ask that all people in the world be kept safe from spiritual and physical danger. I ask that all be in receipt of divine protection. I ask that all be protected from violence, war and aggression. I ask that there be no more war."

Then you ask that all people with the same need as you on the planet be granted the same wish:

"I ask that my prayer be multiplied and sent out to help all of those who are in need of protection on the planet."

Then express gratitude. Example for Michael: "I thank you for all of the protection that you have shown me so far in life. I am truly grateful for not being laid off last month when the company was in financial trouble and for being protected from the gossip of the lady next door."

Then you ask that the request be fulfilled quickly: "I ask that this be done, helping all and harming none. I ask that my request be filled in this hour in full power according to the will of ____." (Insert appropriate name here—God, The I Am That I Am, The Divine Imagination, The Great Being of Light.)

Then say **Amen, or Thank You**.

You may also follow this prayer with a Psalm or a favorite inspirational poem. Read it three to fifteen times.

Be Careful What You Pray For

OK, here comes another big cliché. Be careful what you pray for, because you just might get it.

A good example is the person who thinks that they will get more money if they pray for more work. Instead of money, you might just get more work. I am always getting more work when what I need is higher paying work! Try to be as specific as possible in your phrasing.

Also be very careful when you pray for another. What you believe to be in that person's higher interest may not actually be the best thing for that person. For instance to pray that "Harry stops drinking" might actually be a bit of a curse, if what Harry needs to do is keep drinking until he hits bottom and realizes that he needs help. Harry could quit drinking, but you might have helped delay him from learning a big soul lesson.

The universe also does not like control freaks. No matter how much you, the Bible and all your friends think you are in the right, the Great Wheel of Time corrects karma at the right time and at the right place. It is typically emotions such as fear, hate, envy, jealousy and resentment that drive a control freak to demand that the angels punish another person. In this case, the angels tend to lead the negative prayer to a situation that reflects their lack of compassion back to them. Angels are not instruments of karma, but they can hold up mirrors that reflect the possible outcomes of your actions.

Angels can help you change another's mind about a matter. It depends on your motivation for presenting the request in the first place. If your motivation is to get revenge or control another person's free will, you might be in for a nasty surprise. You see, you are not the only one who can access an angel. Your negative request will merely be processed by your angel and delivered to the other person's angel who will transmute it into positive energy. This is why so many bad people seem to thrive despite all the bad vibes you may be sending them. It is also why, at times, there seems to be no justice in this world. These people are literally living off the transmuted negative energy sent to them by the people they have hurt. This is one of the reasons why, when you pray, it is very important to keep your feelings out of it. If you feel an enormous amount of hate for instance, it may simply be sent to the other person as an enormous amount of love. You have better things to do in life than behave like a large battery that constantly recharges your oppressors with transmuted angelic energy.

Angels also tend to ignore those who are obsessed or ask for the same goal again and again. An example is "Please bring my lover back to me." Once again, this type of request smacks of effort and is a request to control another's free will. Also, if incorrectly sent, the other person often feels this energy like a beach ball that floats further away on a wave each time they try to recover it. The angels don't honor requests that are an insult or violation of the other person's Soul Freedom, no matter how much of a jerk the other person has been to you.

When in doubt, remember this credo: "Pray unto others as you would have them pray unto you."

Visualization

While you pray it can be helpful to practice visualization. Some find this more difficult than others, and others take to visualization better than they do to finding the right words. Visualization is optional, but these are just some suggestions to enhance your experience.

The most basic visualization you can do is imagine the room filled with the colors of light associated with the angel. Or you can imagine your aura filled with the color of that particular angel's light. For instance, if you are praying to the Archangel Chamuel, you could begin by practicing the Higher Self Sun meditation exercise, and imagine that the Fountain of Light you are creating is filled with pink, rose and red sparkles. Or imagine your aura filled with a pink rosy glow.

You may also concentrate on a chakra that is associated with the angel. For instance, the Archangel Chamuel is associated with the heart's center. You may imagine your heart's center blossoming with a pink light or glowing a glamorous emerald green. Or you could imagine a bright emerald green center surrounded by a rose pink glow. Use your imagination and whatever feels right to you.

Another effective exercise is to imagine positive outcomes while you are praying. If you are asking for more money in the bank, picture yourself jumping for joy as you see a bank slip written for the appropriate amount. If you are asking to be reunited with a friend, picture the two of you embracing as you see each other on the street. There is much debate about the role visualization plays in prayer, but I think it helps the angels "get the picture."

Remember a picture can be worth a thousand words, so keep it positive.

Repetition

The human voice is an instrument that can be used to create a trance-like state and help you enhance your connection to the angelic realms. This is called an *incantation*. Remember that what you are repeating here is a Psalm or a prayer and not your own request.

Repetition may also help teach you to breathe correctly. It forces you to breathe from the diaphragm, as one cannot repeat a prayer up to fifteen times using only the larynx, or breathe from the lungs without getting signals from the body like shortness of breath or a sore throat. The simplest incantations are the "aum" or "aaaahh" sounds that are used to initiate Buddhist meditations. Traditionally, "aaaah" is used to open yourself to energy and "auumm" is used to bring energy into manifestation or reality. Sound has been used for centuries to call on the assistance of Higher Powers.

This is optional, but I highly recommend choosing a poem or a prayer that is suitable to your needs and reading it three to fifteen times after you complete each prayer request. In the sections that deal with each Archangel I will recommend suitable Psalms from the Bible that may help you achieve your goal. You may, however, use a prayer from any sacred or religious text. Just the act of repeating these ancient and holy words, that millions before you have read, is said to open the portals to the heavenly realms.

Candle Burning

Lighting a candle is not necessary to access the energy of an angel, but it does help you relax and focus on the goal. Lighting a candle is a formality that has been used for centuries to access Higher Powers and as a tool for prayer. I think you are just as likely to contact an angel sitting on a rock by a stream or while doing the dishes.

The size or shape of the candle does not matter (for instance a large candle does not have more power than a tiny birthday candle), but it is always a good idea to try to use a color that is associated with the particular Archangel. For instance, it is best to use a green candle to access Archangel Raphael or a pink or red one to access the Archangel Chamuel. It is always OK to use a white candle if you cannot find the appropriately colored candle or don't have another color handy. A white candle contains all the colors of the Divine Rainbow.

A flickering flame can help induce a state of meditation. When you first light the candle, stare at it a few minutes and try to empty your mind of all thoughts. Then begin your prayer. After your prayer is over, it is OK to put out the candle and relight it again if you wish. Traditionalists may want to keep the candle burning, as is the tradition in the Catholic Church and in certain white witch circles, but it is not necessary. The burning of the "eternal" flame over a number of days is thought to keep the energy suspended around you. The classic number of days to keep a candle perpetually burning is three, seven or nine. However, there is no need to persistently knock at heaven's gate using the energy generated by a candle unless you feel that it is part of your religion. Fussing over a candle that is supposed to be kept lit for a number of days can rapidly turn into the focus of the exercise when the focus is supposed to be on the angelic energy. That is called mistaking the vessel of the spirit for the spirit itself. Never leave a burning candle unattended.

The traditional candle burning colors for each angel are:

Michael—blue or white
Gabriel—white, yellow, orange or gold

Chamuel—pink or red
Uriel—gold, silver, purple or red
Raphael—green
Jophiel—yellow, orange or gold
Zadkiel—purple or violet

As Linus from Charlie Brown said, "It is better to light a single candle than curse the darkness."

What If There Is No Answer?

If you have been making requests of an angel for months and there is still no solution to the problem manifesting in your life, then one of three things may be happening.

1. You are making an unreasonable request. For instance, if you are sixty-five and demanding to be a pop star with a number-one selling record, chances are your request won't be granted. Keep your wishes within the realm of possibility, even though "with God all things are possible."

2. Intervention in your life by the angels at this time may be costing you a valuable lesson. Many people ask for money when they don't have jobs, for instance. Or they ask for the return of a partner, when the partner is obviously not interested. From what I have seen and heard, the angels do sometimes practice a kind of tough love, forcing you to realize such classic axioms as "you don't get what you want, you get what you need" or "the key to happiness is letting go." This is what the Christians mean when they talk about being drop-kicked by Jesus to the goalpost. The angels will do the same.

3. This may sound cryptic but the lack of an answer may be the answer. The Angels may consider

something that you consider to be a problem or a loss to actually be a blessing. This is particularly true of many relationship requests or those pining over a lost job or opportunity. A "no" from the angels might just mean that there is a silver lining in that cloud hanging over your head.

In general, if you don't have an answer to your problem within three months, you can safely assume that there is no answer and for some reason you are supposed to live with the situation. It is important that you not take this as rejection from the angels. An angel doesn't take things personally like you do. You just have to trust that the universe is unfolding in its own time, and in its own way and just as it should. Giving up the "fight" to get what you want at this point also might be a good idea. The angels do bless those who find themselves in a state of surrender or unconditional bliss.

Peace Be Still

If you want to channel the angels, you have to first be a clear conduit for the information. I am fond of Paramahansa Yoganada's somewhat corny, yet accurate description of the human psyche as a radio that can be tuned to pick up different frequencies.

Most of us are tuned to chaotic frequencies created by our busy minds and bodies. Our psyches are full of the static interference that is created by other people's demands, deadlines, anxieties and problems. Too much television, radio, drugs, alcohol and loud music also serve to shorten our psychic bandwidths. The result is astral chaos that constantly confuses our inner guides and sends us down the wrong path again and again.

The angels vibrate at a certain frequency and one of the best ways to "tune" into them is to learn how to develop a quality of stillness. The Buddhists also call this "a state of mindfulness." In this state, you are aware, but you are also focused. The best way to achieve this state is by practicing meditation, yoga or spending time in nature.

Your psyche can also be compared to a pool. This pool is a mirror and it is in this pool that you will see messages from angels. If the pool is constantly disturbed, rocked by waves of misfortune or stirred by turbulent emotions and violent messages from the real world, it will never be still enough for you to see the images reflected in its depths. Achieving this kind of stillness is easier said than done, and many spend a lifetime trying to achieve this state of sentient bliss.

Still, I have found a simple shortcut to still the pain of a troubled heart and slow down a speeding brain. Before you pray simply take your left hand and place it over your heart and then your right hand and fold it over your left. Say out loud "Peace! Be Still." Then take a deep breath.

Sometimes, if you just tell yourself what to do, you will do it. This seems deceptively simple but it works to help you get out of self and, at least for a few minutes, be a perfect mirror. You become one with God. You realize that God is both the gift and the giver. You are in the present.

Chapter Three

The Angels Within

The Angels Within are your chakras—the seven divine flames or rays that have their own place in your physical body. These centers are often seen as fiery balls, lotus blossoms or wheels of angelic light.

Each of the chakras corresponds to a certain angelic vibration or frequency of light that can be enhanced by creative visualization. The health of these chakras corresponds to the health of your etheric body. These chakras can also be perceived as the homes of the angelic entities.

Periodic opening, clearing and spinning of the chakras can increase your overall attractiveness to the angels.

Opening, Cleansing and Closing the Chakras

Opening the chakras can be visualized in many ways. Some compare the opening of a chakra to the opening of a camera aperture, or the blossoming of a flower. Others see them as small burning suns or like light bulbs that slowly emit a warmer and stronger ray of light as the chakra opens up. Use the visualization that works best for you.

This visualization is best done flat on your back, lying on the bed or on the floor. You can do this exercise in its entirety or you can concentrate on the one chakra that is related to the ray or archangel you want to work with. Some may want to start with only one chakra as this visualization is a bit like that Las Vegas act where the man spins several plates on poles and tries to keep them all in balance.

*

The First Ray, or first or base chakra, connects with issues of survival, procreation, love and will. It is located at the base of your body in the area between your genitals and your anus and is thought to connect to the base of the spine. This area is literally called "the seat of your soul." To find it, simply sit in a chair. Whatever part of your anatomy you are sitting on is essentially your base chakra.

Once you have found this point, imagine it as a pure ruby red color. Imagine the reddest red you can imagine—for example a crimson red. I have found it helpful to imagine the chakra first as a gemstone, like a Burmese ruby, and then imagine it filled with liquid fire. Others have success with imagining the heating elements of a stove or a drop of blood.

To open this chakra, first see the color and then picture the bud of a red flower whose petals are closed over a gem. Picture the buds of the flower slowly opening to reveal a brilliant ruby inside.

As you inhale, imagine this gem being energized and becoming brighter. As it energizes it begins to emanate a glow and warmth that slowly spreads through your pelvis and up towards your belly button as the petals of the blossom slowly unfold.

Now imagine the buds of this flower unfolding until the flower is completely open. The petals of this flower are like rays of light that extend to every part of your body, inside and out.

Now imagine a thread or cord of white light that extends to the heavens and energizes this flower to spin in a clockwise direction.

You are now connected to the Archangels Chamuel, Michael, Gabriel and Raphael who can help you find your life's direction, make major decisions and strengthen your health.

With each breath imagine the thread energizing the ruby red center of this chakra and picture it beginning to spin in a clockwise direction. Keep it spinning.

*

Now I want you to move to a spot about three inches below your belly button. This is your second chakra or the Second Ray. It is classically imagined as a brilliant orange light. Once again, imagine a bud that slowly opens to reveal a sparkling gem inside. Many achieve this by conceiving first a small sun with orange flames for petals. Picture the bud of this flower slowly unfurling its fiery petals and imagine the golden-orange core at its center spreading its warmth through your body. As you inhale, the orange center of the flower becomes more luminous.

Now imagine the thread of white light extending once again to Heaven and energizing the center of this flower. As it does this, see the flower spinning in a clockwise direction—like a small, hurling orange sun.

You are now connected to the energies of the Archangels Zadkiel, Uriel, Jophiel and Chamuel who deal with issues of acceptance, intuition and finding day to day happiness.

Keep this flower spinning.

*

Now, turn your concentration to your stomach area, just beneath your breastbone. This is known as the Third Ray or stomach chakra. It is traditionally imagined as a bright yellow or flaming gold.

Once again, picture a bud whose petals slowly unfurl to reveal a golden center. This pinpoint is like a diamond that emanates a golden light that spreads warmth throughout your belly and chest cavity. Each time you inhale, this diamond grows brighter and brighter, warming and comforting your chest and stomach area.

The thread of white light extends once more to heaven and as it does this, imagine the flower spinning in a clockwise direction, like a flaming wheel of light—a mini-sun.

You are now connecting to the energies of the Archangels Michael, Gabriel, Jophiel, Uriel, Chamuel and Zadkiel who deal with such issues as our shadow selves, our sense of identity, mothering and fathering issues and attachments to others.

Keep this flaming sunflower spinning.

*

Your heart's center, or the Fourth Ray, is situated where your heart is… although some people picture it aligned with the other chakras in a straight line up the spine. Either visualization is OK.

This chakra is traditionally associated with the color green. Imagine a dark forest green—the deepest green you can imagine at the center of your heart. If that is not working for you it is OK to imagine a red or rose-colored flower, also associated with this ray. But technically the Fourth Ray is the color of healing and growth—green.

Picture the petals of this bud unfolding to reveal a tiny pinpoint of light that resembles a sparkling green emerald. As the petals unfold and you breathe in, the emerald is energized and becomes liquid fire. As you continue to breathe in, imagine the warmth from this gem expanding and filling your chest cavity with its glorious green light.

As the emerald grows brighter and brighter, picture a thread or cord of golden or silver light extending to the heavens. Energized by this light, the petals of this flower begin to spin in a clockwise direction.

You are now connected to the energies of the Archangels Michael, Raphael and Jophiel who deal with issues of the heart: connecting to others, surrendering and letting go and healing and achieving harmony in life.

Keep the flower in your heart chakra spinning.

*

Now find the place at your throat where your thyroid would be. This is the Fifth Ray, also known as the throat chakra. The color associated with this chakra is blue. Imagine any shade of blue that appeals to you… a sky blue, the stormy blue of an ocean.

Now imagine a radiant blue bud. The petals of this bud open to reveal a shining point of light, a small blue star that glints like a sapphire at its center. As you breathe in, this star becomes brighter until it pulsates with an intense laser-blue light and the petals of the flower unfold. Some of you will see flowers with several petals. Others will picture millions of petals. Visualize these petals unfurling until the flower is open and glowing in all of its glory.

Now imagine the cord, thread or beam of light connecting you to the heavens, and as you do so, imagine the chakra beginning to spin in a clockwise direction.

You are now connected to the energies of the Archangel Michael, Uriel and Zadkiel who deal with issues of self-expression, confidence, autonomy, intelligence and the ability to learn from mistakes.

Keep this chakra spinning.

*

The next chakra is located at the Third Eye and is called the Sixth Ray or the Sixth Chakra. Its color is magenta or indigo, which are dark violet tones. Imagine the colors of twilight or dawn and you will find the correct shade of purple. Eggplant is also an appropriate color for this chakra.

Visualize a dark purple flower at the place between your brows. The petals slowly unfurl to reveal a violet diamond inside that becomes brighter each time you inhale. This particular diamond, though violet, also at times emanates the entire spectrum of the rainbow.

As you breathe in, picture the petals unfolding and this gem energizing and releasing a rainbow that surrounds you in a halo of light extending three feet in either direction. For some people this chakra also manifests in showers of gold.

Now imagine a cord or beam of light reaching directly to the heavens and the chakra spinning in a clockwise direction. It is a wheel of purple fire.

You are now in connection with the Archangels Michael, Jophiel, Uriel and Zadkiel. They are concerned with such issues as illumination, spiritual wisdom, guidance and awareness, intuitive abilities, karma, soulmates, balance, ideals and universal ideals.

Keep this blossom spinning.

*

At the top of your head is the crown chakra that is also known as the Seventh Ray or the Seat of Enlightenment. This chakra is associated with the thousand petals of the lotus although you may picture whatever flower feels right to you.

Picture this flower sitting like a hat at the crown of your head. It is a light pink or light violet color. Picture thousands of petals unfolding until you see the center of the blossom. This is a diamond-like gem that emits pink and violet rays. Each time you breathe in this gem is energized until it forms a ball of liquid fire, becoming brighter and brighter until it resembles a miniature sun, glowing in the center.

Now imagine a stream of bright white light connecting your crown chakra to the heavens.

You are now connected to the energies of Zadkiel, Gabriel, Michael and Uriel. These angels are concerned with issues of divine guidance, potential, intuition and Soul Freedom.

Keep this chakra spinning.

*

Imagine each chakra, one by one, filled or rinsed with a brilliant white light.

At the end of this exercise, it is important to close each of your chakras, one by one, by picturing the bud closing and embracing the gem. At the conclusion of the exercise place your hands over your heart and say "Peace Be Still."

This visualization is so involved that many automatically find themselves in a state of surrender ideal for meditation. This exercise is formatted to help you heal from the inside out—it is a bit of a fallacy that help actually comes from outside ourselves. The angels do live within you. Each of our chakras is like a hologram that contains all of the energies that create the entire Divine Rainbow.

Chapter Four

The Angels Above

The Archangel Chamuel—The Angel of Love

"Live and Let Live" is the holy decree of this angel who is concerned with the state of surrender as a state of bliss. Chamuel teaches us both acceptance and unconditional love—of the self and of others. This angel is about the paradox of Soul Freedom and your right to live your life the way you want without interference from others.

If there is one thing this angel seems to abhor, it is a control freak. Chamuel teaches us lessons about letting go. He teaches us to let others make their own mistakes without interference, anxiety and fuss from us. He also helps us understand why others reflect anxiety and misery onto us, and how to change our behavior accordingly.

Chamuel is the angel to reach out to if you find yourself in conflict with friends or family. He inspires mercy, compassion and forgiveness in hearts that are closed to the possibility of reconciliation. He can facilitate the dissipation of the ego, and dissolve feelings of greed, vanity, envy and lust. He can also save us from unhealthy attachments to people and things that we feel belong to us. He teaches us that love is earned, not owed, and that happiness is not a goal, but a state of being. Chamuel melts hearts that have been frozen with regret or longing to live in another time and teaches us to live in the present. He encourages us to "love the one you're with."

Chamuel, who is related to the base chakra, can teach us to align our hearts with our will, and then align that with the Divine Imagination. He is the angel of kindness, tenderness and also human intimacy. He is the angel to pray to if you are having sexual problems or having trouble magnetizing a partner to you.

It is said we can't love others until we learn to love ourselves first. Chamuel's rosy pink rays are said to cleanse hearts of resentment, recrimination and harsh self- talk. His green rays are thought to heal battered bodies and spirits. He is the angel that can sweeten sour memories and repair a damaged relationship. His light is fiery, yet fluid, and promotes the free circulation of love amongst groups of people. Chamuel is also the angel to pray to if you want to be introduced to new friends and kindred spirits. He dispels prejudice, racial biases and protects individuals against slander, malice, gossip and loss of reputation.

Chamuel is also concerned with your survival on a practical level. He is the angel that facilitates financial opportunities and gifts. He can also help you find lost objects or restore that which is stolen back to its rightful owner.

Chamuel (sometimes pronounced Samuel) is often thought to appear in a glaze of pink and gold light, or in a rose bubble. He was thought to be the angel who reassured Christ of a resurrection while he was on the cross. You are sure to find Chamuel and his angels anywhere where there is rushing or flowing water, whether it is in the overflowing banks of the Nile or a babbling mountain stream.

Physically Chamuel is connected to the sexual organs, the circulatory system, the heart and the sense of touch.

Light a pink, red, green or gold candle to connect to the energies of Chamuel. His gemstone is the ruby, or rose quartz and his metals are iron and gold. He is connected to the First Ray and the base or sacral chakra.

Psalms related to Chamuel are Psalm 20 (for heavenly blessings), Psalm 47 (to find love each day), Psalm 53 (for instilling love in the heart), Psalm 54 (to master one's negative thoughts) and Psalm 98 (to keep a happy heart and a joyful attitude).

A mantra you can use to call on Chamuel at any time is:

I call Archangel Chamuel
And his Angels of Love
Manifest right conditions
As below, so above.

The Archangel Jophiel—The Angel of Illumination

"Know thyself" is Archangel Jophiel's holy decree. Jophiel is the angel to turn to if you are having trouble digesting your experiences or finding yourself making the same mistakes again and again. Jophiel also aids those who suffer from low self-esteem or who are the victims of other people's ignorant behavior. Jophiel teaches you not to take things personally and to rise above inappropriate behavior, conflicts and challenges. Jophiel can also protect you from arrogant people, false gurus and those poisoned by spiritual pride.

Jophiel takes care of those whose minds have been blown, either by addiction or a traumatic experience. He is the one to pray to when you feel like your aura has been shattered or that you can't possibly go on one more minute. As the Angel of the Twelve Steps, he is the one to pray to if you find yourself dealing with an alcoholic, addict or mentally ill individual. He also helps those with damaged instincts reconnect to their Higher Self. If you are having trouble getting with a program, this is the angel to call upon for assistance.

Ever heard the phrase "Pride goeth before a fall"? If the universe seems to be tripping you up every time you make a firm pronouncement about the future, Jophiel is probably behind the booby-trap trying to tell you something. This angel is also connected with the concept of *satori*—the dawning of divine spiritual realization that finds you aware of what a gift it is to live in the present.

You can call upon Jophiel for practical assistance with such matters as studying, absorbing information and passing a test. Jophiel's brilliant yellow and orange light is also thought to be the fountain of inspiration for artists, writers, scientists and inventors.

Physically, Jophiel takes care of the digestion system, liver, kidney and ears, and one's sense of balance. Jophiel, spelt sometimes as Iofiel, is thought to be associated with the planet Saturn. Like Saturn, Jophiel forces people to face up to and overcome their personal limitations. Jophiel, who is sometimes seen as one of the angels of a thousand eyes, is also believed to be the angel that herded Adam and Eve out of the Garden of Eden.

His metal is copper and his gemstone is citrine. His domain is cities, and in particular, Jophiel is said to be fond of older architecture, especially in universities, churches and libraries.

To connect with Jophiel, light a yellow candle, which is thought to correspond with his fiery light, or an orange candle, which connects the angel to your second chakra.

Psalms that relate to Jophiel are: Psalm 32 (when sorry for sins), Psalm 56 (to overcome temptation),

Psalm 89 (for acceptance of events) Psalm 99 (for purity), Psalm 107 (to control addiction), Psalm 124 (to overcome temptation) and Psalm 102 (to receive healing rays).

A quick call to Jophiel is:
I call Archangel Jophiel
And his Angels of Divine Right
I pray for right conditions
Manifest now the light.

The Archangel Gabriel—The Angel of Guidance

"You have nothing to fear but fear itself" is the decree of this angel. However it could be amended to "You have nothing to fear but yourself." The Archangel Gabriel teaches us to embrace the darkest parts of ourselves and the shadow sides of our personalities. It is this shadow side that is thought to constantly draw negative experiences and energies to us. Many of you have experienced the phenomenon where, shortly after criticizing another, you find yourself criticized about the exact same flaw by somebody else. That is the Archangel Gabriel's sense of humor at work.

Connecting to Gabriel's holy light is thought to purify and rinse the etheric body of negative emotions and feelings transferred to you from another person. His home in your body is the third chakra or solar plexus, which is the center that connects us astrally to others. He is in charge of our gut instincts and intuition, and helps us be wise in our judgement.

Gabriel is the grand social convener. The third chakra, above all other chakras, is known as the seat of the personality and is the most vulnerable to astral attack. Obsessed people, people with personality disorders, alcoholics, addicts, codependents, control freaks and women with battered wife syndrome often find themselves wrestling with the Archangel Gabriel on a full-time basis. If you find you possess any of the above disorders, then you would be better off to regard Gabriel as your personal PR assistant than as an energy that keeps you from "what you want." Gabriel can teach you to let go of people and situations that are unhealthy or bad for you.

Have you ever felt poisoned by the energies of another person? Do you constantly find yourself invaded or pushed around by angry, fearful, aggressive or controlling energies? Gabriel is the angel that can help you reform these relationships or detach from them completely. The energy of Gabriel can heal or replace gut instincts that have been injured by abusive childhoods, violence and traumatic stress. Gabriel is the light that you can take with you in the most challenging of situations and environments.

Gabriel is also the angel to pray to if you have done something wrong or find yourself in a fix that you don't know how to get out of. His light is associated with daybreak and the dawn of realization (*satori*).

Gabriel is the beacon of light at the end of a long, dark, personal tunnel. If you are feeling depressed, discouraged, lonely, disconnected from others, picked on, the butt of a cosmic joke, dissatisfied or just plain lost in life, Gabriel is the one who can help you find your way out of the darkness. Gabriel also assists seekers in finding their correct spiritual path. He is one of the few angels that deals expressly with putting emotions and reactions in their proper places. Spiritually, Gabriel is the Grand Architect who rebuilds shattered souls and broken lives.

Practically, Gabriel can help you with the following mundane details: making to-do lists and long-term plans, scheduling, cleanliness, discipline and organization. He can make time accelerate or seem like it is standing still. He is also the angel to pray to if you are trying to achieve a long-term practical goal such as losing weight or saving money.

Gabriel is also related to the phrase "playing to win." He can turn wallflowers into brides and dyslexics into university professors. He helps students with their studies and guides mentors: when the student is ready, it is Gabriel who often brings the teacher. Pray to Gabriel for "right conditions" to bring you success in any endeavor.

Gabriel is fond of butterflies and sunshine and can be seen in the reflection of sunlight in the water. His gemstones are the yellow topaz and the diamond. Carrying a yellow topaz is thought to prevent healers and psychics from picking up negative energies from toxic clients. When you feel like you have been punched in the gut, or like you have butterflies in your stomach, that is Gabriel warning you of a momentous event.

Historically, Gabriel is seen as the angel of annunciation, mercy, vengeance, death and revelation. Mohammed describes him in the Koran as having one hundred and forty pairs of wings. In Jewish legend, it was Gabriel who was thought to have brought destruction upon the cities of Sodom and Gomorrah.

Physically, Gabriel is in charge of eyesight, ears, fingers, legs and the stomach. He can help you digest experiences.

Gabriel is the Angel of Connecting to Others. To connect to him light a yellow, white or gold candle. He is the Third Ray and connects to the solar plexus.

Suggested Psalms for repetition are: Psalm 20 (when in distress), Psalm 32 (when sorry), Psalm 38 (to lose all fear and anxiety), Psalm 55 (for guidance), Psalm 99 (when feeling desolate and lonely) and Psalm 142 (when in distress).

You can call on Gabriel at any tme by reciting this quick mantra:

I call Archangel Gabriel
And his guiding Beings of Light
Please light my path and show my way
Out of this soul's dark night.

The Archangel Raphael—The Angel of Healing and Harmony

Raphael's key phrase is "As Above, So Below." He is the angel that dances in harmony with the cosmic spheres and makes sure that things in your personal universe are unfolding as they should at the right time. If you are feeling disturbed, discombobulated, misrepresented and misunderstood, Raphael is the angel to pray to for some clarity.

Raphael is associated with the Karmic Wheel, also known as the Great Wheel of Time. He takes care of our physical, spiritual and social cycles. He helps us understand that we can't freeze time and that to everything there is a season and a reason—a beginning and end.

Raphael is the Fourth Ray and corresponds to the heart's center. When your heart is broken, he is the angel to pray to for the power to forgive your oppressor and for acceptance of the situation. He teaches us to love unconditionally, with no thought of vengeance or reward.

If there is discord at home or at work, Raphael is the angel who can help you restore peace and harmony in your surroundings. He takes care of demanding bosses, fighting kids and unpleasant neighbors. He also loves a clean house. His spirit is often sensed in gardens and in other places of landscaped beauty.

Raphael is the Master of Music and Mathematics, and is believed to dance with the divine spheres. If you are in need of good timing, ask Raphael to throw a little serendipity your way. He is influential with Venus and the Three Fates. The source of most unhappiness comes from a longing for a time when one was in love with someone else. Raphael is a Houdini that can help you escape this trap by helping you "love the one you're with."

If you are suffering from the kind of tunnel vision that comes from repeatedly trying to force your will on people and events, Raphael can help you widen your horizons. He teaches those who are stubborn to think outside the box. He hands people the golden key to their own emotional prisons. A heart that is closed to the world is closed to luck and opportunity.

Raphael is also the angel of unconditional surrender to events. He restores faith to those whose hearts have lost it in others. He teaches us to put our faith in ourselves and our own Higher Powers instead of in fools on Earth.

Raphael restores wholeness to body, mind and spirit. He corresponds to all of the circulatory systems in your body, and to the circulation of money in your life. If you find yourself poverty stricken, Raphael is the angel to pray to, to keep food on the table and cash in the bank. He rules anything that is fluid: time, emotions and rites of passage. He thaws out frozen hearts and clears the cells of the kind of resentment that can cause cancer. He removes those blocks that are preventing the free circulation of love, positive energy and money in our lives.

Traditionally, Raphael is the angel that is asked to heal all afflictions and disorders of the body, but he is especially known for helping with diseases of the heart and circulatory system.

Historically, Raphael is thought to be the Guardian of the Tree of Life in the Garden of Eden and the angel who handed Noah a medical book after the great flood. He was also thought to have handed King Solomon a magic, five-pointed star ring, to protect him from demons while he built his famous temple.

You are likely to find Raphael anywhere that you find a deep end, such as the bottom of the ocean or at the base of volcanoes. His voice is also thought to be heard singing in the sap of the trees in the spring and in the positive ions after a rainstorm.

Raphael also corresponds to the Fourth Ray, which is identified by a deep emerald green, but as he is often identified with the heart, his colors are also rose and pink. His gemstones are the emerald, dioptase, chysoprase, rose quartz and pink topaz. Light a rose, pink or green candle to help you connect to the energies of this magnificent angelic being.

Suggested Psalms for repetition are: Psalm 3 (to have a nice day), Psalm 7 (for health), Psalm 26 (for help with finances), Psalm 47 (to find love each and every day), Psalm 53 (to instill love in the heart), Psalm 60 (to leave the past behind), Psalm 98 (to keep a happy heart and a joyful attitude) and Psalm 166 (for physical recovery).

A short mantra you can use to call Raphael is:
I call Archangel Raphael
And his angels of Healing Light
Strengthen my mind, body and soul
With inspiration, spirit and might.

The Archangel Michael—The Angel of Protection and Truth

"The Truth shall set you free" is the decree of this angel. If you or are lost in a jungle of any kind, Michael's sword can untangle you from your forest of delusions. Michael is also related to the phrase, "We have nothing to fear but fear itself." He strips away the veils of illusion with his fiery sword.

Part of feeling safe in life is knowing that we only make decisions that are truly in our own best interests. Michael is the angel to turn to when you feel pushed around by others, emotionally terrorized, or somehow invaded by another person's presence. Michael can help you regain control of your life.

Michael can also help you banish your inner critic and free you from fear of the future. This angel strengthens your faith in your self, especially when it comes to the faith that you can handle whatever obstacle Fate throws your way. He also represents virtues that are sometimes called the Keys of Heaven: repentance, righteousness, mercy and sanctification.

Externally, Michael is thought to protect individuals from all physical and spiritual aggression including accidents, diseases, crime, astral attacks and the evil eye. He is the angel to pray to if you feel you are being treated unfairly at work, have made a huge mistake and need to have it fixed or feel that you are the victim of another person's addiction, mental illness or injustice.

In Jewish, Christian and Islamic writings, Michael ranks as one of the greatest of all angels. In Christian imagery he is often depicted carrying an unsheathed sword. This is the sword of righteousness that slays both inner and outer dragons and demons. The Muslims give him quite another appearance: he is a creature with emerald wings covered in saffron hairs. Each of these hairs contains a million faces and as many mouths and tongues. He is also thought to be the fire that Moses saw in the burning bush. One of his heavenly responsibilities is to weigh souls at the time of death.

Michael, the Fifth Ray in the divine rainbow, is often associated with a steely blue or laser blue light. In cases of emergency, surrounding yourself in a bubble of this blue light is thought to offer protection. Explosive in his actions, Michael is thought to be related to thunder and lightning. When you get news that seems like "a bolt from the blue," often Michael is behind it. Michael also likes mirrors. He is also the angel who reflects your own actions back to you. His miracles tend to occur swiftly and suddenly. Known for his sense of humor, Michael is related to the phrase "humor destroys all karma."

Michael is also thought to like heights. People believe they are most connected to him when standing at the peak of a mountain, the top of a skyscraper or in an airplane. He is fond of flight and is thought to inspire spontaneous instances of bilocation (where the same person is seen in two places at once). He likes anything metal and his gemstone is the sapphire.

It is thought he guides the blades of surgeons and physicians. Physically, he takes care of the heart, tongue, mouth, thyroid, endocrine system, liver and heart. He is also connected to hearing and perspective.

When you meditate, see Michael corresponding to your throat chakra, which is your seat of self-expression. To connect with Michael, it is suggested you light a blue candle.

Psalms associated with Michael and his Angels of Protection are: Psalm 3 (to conquer all fears), Psalm 6 and 7 (for protection), Psalm 10 (for protection and help), Psalm 12 (against oppression), Psalm 11 (triumph over adversities), Psalm 17 (for justice), Psalm 28 (for protection against the wicked), Psalm 64 (for protection), Psalm 70 (for help), Psalm 83 (to ward off enemies) and Psalm 85 (of which Michael is thought to be the author).

A quick call that you can use to access the protection of Michael is:

I call on Archangel Michael
And his Angels of Protection
Protect me now from all that harms
And restore my life's perfection!

The Archangel Uriel—The Angel of Peace

The Archangel Uriel, also known as the Angel of Letting Go and Selfless Service, is a truly majestic being whose credo is reflected in the phrase "to rule is to serve." Uriel instills a sense of courage and trust in our Higher Selves. He teaches us to love others no matter what they do to us.

Uriel teaches us not to take things personally and to respect the paths or journeys that other people have chosen. If you are not sure of your own path, Uriel, who relates to the Third Eye, can help you develop a vision quest. This incredible angel is aligned with the Aquarian ideals of divine justice, non-exclusivity, complete faith and the promotion of peace and understanding. Uriel's relationship to the Third Eye, and the opening of that eye in order to see the truth, or have the truth presented to you by others, has him closely related to Buddhist ideas about enlightenment and becoming one with a Higher Power. He is also the angel responsible for visionary or inspirational states of mind and is said to bestow bliss on those who can totally let go of all preconceptions and illusions about the past, present and future. For this reason, I choose to call him the Angel of Meditation.

If you are feeling restless or perturbed, Uriel is who you should call on to restore your sense of inner tranquility. He restores faith to disappointed idealists and inspires poets, musicians and artists to create visions of beauty. He teaches us to see eternity in a grain of sand. Uriel is also identified with altered states of religious ecstasy like *satori* (the dawning of consciousness) and *shakti* (the manifestation of an idea into reality.) Ask Uriel to present you with choices if you feel trapped or can't seem to alter a disastrous chain of events.

By letting go of emotions, opinions and prejudices we learn to surrender to the path we find ourselves put on. If you don't like the cards that Fate has dealt you, Uriel can teach you how to play them to win.

If you find yourself in conflict with others, Uriel can help you arrive at a peaceful resolution. He resolves disputes of all kinds and facilitates the manifestation of divine justice on all levels.

He is associated with the phrase "The key to happiness is letting go." Uriel is the Angel that teaches you that life is "not about you." Whether you are a Christian or Buddhist you can identify with the concept that life is somehow pre-formatted, and that often, you don't have a choice about what happens to you. Uriel is the angel to pray to for help when you feel completely powerless over the evolution of events.

Uriel is also the Angel of the Wounded Healer and inspires those in recovery to go out and help others find their way out of distress and illusion. He also provides inspiration for any occupation that has to do with caregiving: doctors, teachers, crisis-line workers, psychics and intuitives. If you want to increase your psychic abilities, ask Uriel to bless you with second sight.

Historically, Uriel, who is also known as the Flame of God, has been identified as the angel who wrestled with Jacob, and the messenger sent to Noah to warn him of the impending flood. In the Zohar he is described as a flaming serpent. His symbol is an open hand holding a flame.

You are likely to find Uriel's energy sliding into your room on a sunbeam or in the rays of a spectacular sunset.

Physically he corresponds to the eyes, nose, brain, heart and the pituitary gland. His microcosm is the single cell of the body; his macrocosm the sun.

To connect with him light a candle in any one of his colors: magenta, purple, red or gold.

Suggested repetitive Psalms are: Psalm 20 (for heavenly blessings), Psalm 36 (to receive Divine Grace), Psalm 40 (for spiritual grace), Psalm 42 (to enhance psychic abilities), Psalm 50 (to see opportunities for good), Psalm 53 (for wisdom), Psalm 54 (to master negative thoughts), Psalm 78 (to intensify intuition) and Psalm 119 (for understanding).

A short mantra you can use to access the energies of Uriel is:

I call on Arechangel Uriel
And his legions of light and peace.
All that is not mine by divine right
I ask for immediate release!

The Archangel Zadkiel—The Angel of Joy

The glorious tranformative energies of the Archangel Zadkiel teach us that when it comes to spiritual matters, "God is both the gift and the giver. We cannot separate the giver from gift." When it comes to divine love, he will tell you that "You are the lover, the loving and the beloved." He helps us realize that divinity comes from within; a concept that relates to the idea of the I Am That I Am or Christian concepts of Christ Consciousness.

As Zadkiel relates to the crown chakra—which is responsible for receiving divine rays from The Great Being of Light, The Divine Imagination, God or your Higher Self—and is also responsible for teaching you that you are one with that power. He makes miracle workers of ordinary mortals and teaches them how to become angels on Earth who are always guided by a divine light. To be touched by this angel is to be truly blessed.

Zadkiel teaches us that the greatest gift you can give yourself or another is Soul Freedom. Without understanding that concept, we cannot ever be happy or achieve our highest potential.

This concept has two main aspects. First, there is the concept of letting others have their Soul Freedom. This means detaching yourself from all pretenses that you can control another human being or that others somehow owe you a living, an apology, a fifth step or even the return of your love, mercy, compassion or understanding. Zadkiel teaches us that one of the true keys to happiness is to not have expectations of others, and to realize in this life that anything is possible and that anything can happen (bad or good.) You have no choice. You are not meant to chase other people's souls like some kind of demented butterfly catcher. You are not to sit there, playing God and bidding them, in your mind, to do your will. You are to let them go and hope that they will grow into their true potential.

The second aspect has to do with the concept of freeing yourself from your own doubts, fears, pain and negative traits. Most of us live our lives balled up in a spiritual fetal position, surrounded by the warm, secure darkness of our misery. Zadkiel is the angel that encourages us to emerge from this chrysalis and blossom into our full potential as human beings. When the heart is aligned with the will and the Divine Imagination, we become the masters of positive energy. The energies connected to Zadkiel are thought to be so powerful that they can alter the course of events and cause the spontaneous manifestation of needed people or materials.

Connecting to Zadkiel can also help you learn the fine art of psychic transmutation. In this practice, any negative energy that is sent to you is transformed into positive energy. The famous evangelist, Elizabeth Clare Prophet, calls this the "transmutation of the violet flame." The idea is to throw all of our troubles into an imaginary spiral of violet flame to be transformed into golden light.

The violet flame associated with Zadkiel is thought to be so strong that it dissolves all things that are not of itself. In other words, it destroys all Fool's Gold—inventions of the human mind, prejudices, other manifestations of mankind's greedy and lustful imagination, and transforms it into the true treasure of Divine Wisdom. This divine love of the violet flame, of which Zadkiel is the keeper, is thought by great religious figures such as Florence Scovel Shinn, Paramahansa Yogananda and Elizabeth Clare Prophet to resemble a strong chemical dissolving everything that separates a person from his divine self: negative memories, the three Rs (resentment, revenge and retribution), prejudice, the Seven Sins and all energies that can be considered anti-love.

Even if you don't believe it, you have got to love the concept that we are like damaged holograms of a divine creator, and that accessing divine light can assist us in creating a Heaven on Earth.

Historically, Zadkiel is thought to be the angel of forgiveness, mercy and justice. He provides inspiration for all that have created miracles and masterpieces on Earth including architects, artists, engineers, researchers and scientists.

Traditionally, Zadkiel is associated with the bounty of the planet Jupiter (thought to bring blessings to those under its influence.) In the Bible, he is responsible for many incidents of divine intervention, including the staying of Abraham's arm just before he is about to slaughter Isaac on the altar.

Physically, Zadkiel is related to the overall health of the body, but in particular, the health of the invisible bodies of light and energy that are said to surround our gowns of flesh.

Zadkiel loves a party. Another saying that relates to him is that "humor dissolves karma." He is the angel of what Yogananda calls "Smile Millionaires"; people who spread goodwill wherever they go. He can be found wherever spiritual and material riches can be found. Yet his presence is often found in the slimmest and most miserable of circumstances, as darkness often feeds off his light. You can hear his voice in the delighted laugh of a child, and see his beauty in the surrender of the man weeping with resignation in prison.

Zadkiel's gemstone is a clear quartz, which is a stone known for its ability to receive and transmit angelic vibrations. Clear quartz is a prism that reflects all colors of the divine rainbow.

You can connect to Zadkiel by lighting a violet or white candle.

Psalms recommended for repetition are Psalm 5 (promote spiritual growth), Psalm 25 (spiritual enlightenment), Psalm 102 (receive healing rays), Psalm 148 (to praise God) and Psalm 149 (to understand Divine Imagination).

A short joyous call you can use to acknowlegde the energies of Zadkiel is:

I call on Archangel Zadkiel
And his Angels of the Violet Flame
Happiness, joy and right conditions
Are now mine to immediately claim!

Chapter Five

The Divine Rainbow

The Importance of Surrender

Most of us spend all of our time fighting our fate or trying to conquer circumstances that have obviously already conquered us. Often what we see as a necessity is not a necessity at all, but a way of freeing ourselves from burdens and limited circumstances. This is what most religious types call a "crisis of faith."

A friend of mine once wisely commented that "life would go so much better for most of us if we would only surrender or give in to circumstances, rather than fight our fate every inch of the way. So many of us spend our time fighting with what God has planned for us, that we have no idea whether our life would have been better or not, if we had just given up the struggle to have our way."

This friend was referring to the religious principle known as "the pain is in the struggle." We are genuinely skeptical that the Universe is a benign and generous place. Privately most of us believe that we know what is best for us, not God.

Being in a true state of spiritual surrender—which means giving up all skepticism, fear, doubt and dread of the future—is easier said than done, but it is one sure way to send a signal to the angels that you are ready, willing and able to receive their assistance.

The key is to open your heart, mind and soul to the possibility that with the aid of an angel, you can access your own divinity and help yourself.

Wrestling with the Angels

One consequence or side effect of praying to the angels, and perhaps not understanding their messages, is a harmful habit, encounter or situation that repeats itself. This is an angel's subtle way of pointing out to you that you are living in wrong conditions or self-delusion or straying from your life's path. When this happens, it feels like your angels are turning into inner demons, and that perception is not that far from the truth. Every time you lie to an angel, you cause yourself soul damage.

For instance, if you ask Raphael for money, he may send you a windfall, but if you continue to think you can get away with overspending, you will be knocking at his astral door again and again. After a while, Raphael may choose to exaggerate the changes that you need to make in life by creating a situation that makes it necessary for you to change.

If your issue is annoying or pushy people, you might pray to Gabriel to seal off your third chakra, so that you no longer feel invaded by these people. However, if your motivation is to control others or experience the glory of being able to dominate or control others without resistance from them, the Archangel might just send you more irritants than ever to challenge your motivations and show you that you are on the wrong path.

However, the demon that we all wrestle with is the personality and the ego's natural resistance to believing that anything of a supernatural nature could have some control over us. Demons like skepticism, doubt, fear, resistance, desire and lust make us believe we can cheat an angel by asking for one thing and then displaying in real life that we actually want another.

If you find yourself wrestling with an angel, the thing to do is stop. Give up. Give in. Surrender. More than half the time you will find that once you stop fighting for something, the angels will give it to you anyway. However, more than half the time, you also will find that once you get it, you don't want it anymore. If you have a wish come true, and then find out that you didn't really want it in the first place, then what you were wishing for was produced as the result of an attachment to an ego desire. The personality has a natural resistance to the Higher Self and the more you try to negate its desires by shedding angelic light on its shadows, the more you are going to feel like you are in the middle of some kind of Cosmic Boxing Match. This kind of inner conflict can lead to some spectacular falls to rock bottom in life, but also to some spectacular positive life changes that would not have occurred without the ego being defeated.

When in doubt about how to surrender the fight, just decide truly in your heart, "I do not want what I do not have," and all resistance to your ideas usually drops away.

Ecstasy Without Drugs

Many would disagree with me here, especially the big pot smokers, but there is no greater block to the evolution of human consciousness than the use of drugs and alcohol. This includes the modern versions of Aldous Huxley's soma, such as LSD, ecstasy or antidepressants.

My theory is that anything ingested that creates a feeling like euphoria or well-being will not put you on the path to enlightenment, but warmly shroud you in a cocoon of self-delusion. That is because enlightenment, or for that matter, a connection with the angels, has nothing to do with the expression of an emotion. Drugs such as marijuana, LSD and Ecstasy create a false sense of connection to people and things that don't ultimately matter. These substances also pollute the universe with the kind of bad shakti or perverse manifestations that make the angels hide from us in Heaven. The imaginings and illusions created from these false religious experiences create a kind of astral pollution that makes it harder than ever for people to tune into their Higher Selves.

Nothing causes more soul or aura damage than drugs and alcohol. Most of us are born with Divine Vessels that are cosmically as big and wide and deep as Lake Superior. Drug and alcohol experimentation has a way of shrinking that cup to the size of a thimble. No matter how many times you try to fill it up with divine information, it just cannot hold the amount of astral light that you truly need to ascend in this life. You see this effect in long term attendees of AA meetings, who spend three to five days a week praying to fill their cup with spiritual guidance from God. Yet somehow their cups never runneth over. When your Divine Cup is the size of a thimble, you have to keep going back to the meetings again and again to keep yourself spiritually full. You become like a broken hologram that can only reflect the fractured pieces of the I Am That I Am. An ordinary, non-addicted person, however, does not need to resort to supernatural help as they are often capable of absorbing and keeping the information sent to them. In fact, if you are living a life in which you do not feel you have to pray for assistance at all, you are probably close to spiritually perfect!

In the Angelic World, all things are possible. You can create your own serotonin as people did for centuries through yoga, exercise and meditation.

If you truly want to connect to the Divine Imagination, I suggest you put down the wine glass, pot pipe or Paxil and concentrate on relaxing yourself naturally, sending *kundalini* up through your spine and opening your Third Eye.

Get Real! How To Be an Angel on Earth

The definition of an angel on Earth is a person that easily and effortlessly personifies the image of his or her Higher Self. This is the self that was never born, never died and has never known bitterness, rejection, sorrow or doubt. It is the part of you that walks and talks with the angels and never has to strive, reach or grope for anything. It is free of all dis-ease—physical, psychological, emotional and spiritual. This person has become the Gift and the Giver. He or she wants nothing and therefore is not at want for anything.

We have all met such a person. The person is not particularly special or religious, but they are able to uplift others with just a few words or a glance. They seem to be naturally lucky and never get sick. This person radiates divine love. They are the Lover, the Loved and the Beloved. They are able to heal or diminish negative energy with their presence. Think Oprah Winfrey, not Martha Stewart.

To put the Divine Imagination to work in your own life, you have to practice the following: faith, fearlessness, non-resistance and unconditional love. You must integrate the Angels Within with the Angels Above to recharge and energize your being with divine light.

Man does not live on bread alone. He lives on spirit. Without spirit you are the walking wounded, devoid of prana, chi, or divine inspiration. You are like the hollow men of the T.S. Eliot poem. You have no astral signature. You become a vehicle for negative energies.

You are the Divine Director of your own resurrection from Human Fool to Human Angel. The Archangels are your guides to helping you fulfill your higher purpose—creating a Heaven On Earth.

Parting
Thoughts

7 Deadly Social Sins
—Gandhi

1) politics without principle
2) wealth without work
3) commerce without morality
4) pleasure without conscience
5) education without character
6) science without humanity
7) worship without sacrifice

The Paradoxical Commandments
—Kent M. Keith

People are unreasonable, illogical and self-centered.
Love them anyway.

If you do good, people will accuse you of selfish, ulterior motives.
Do good anyway.

If you are successful, you will win false friends and true enemies.
Succeed anyway.

The good you do today will be forgotten tomorrow.
Do good anyway.

Honesty and frankness make you vulnerable.
Be honest and frank anyway.

The biggest person with the biggest ideas can be shot down by the smallest person with the smallest mind.
Think big anyway.

What you spend years building may be destroyed overnight.
Build anyway.

People really need help but may attack if you help them.
Help people anyway.

Give the world the best you have and you might get kicked in the teeth.
Give the world the best you've got anyway.

Indian Proverb
A candle is a protest at midnight.
It is a non-conformist.
It says to the darkness,
I beg to differ.